BLESSED JOHN HENRY NEWMAN
Heart Speaks to Heart

DANIEL SEWARD

BLESSED JOHN HENRY NEWMAN

Heart Speaks to Heart

Illustrations by
Susan Bateman

ST PAULS

Other titles in this series:

St Paul – Friend of Jesus
St Thérèse of Lisieux – The Little Flower
St John Vianney – The Curé of Ars

ST PAULS Publishing
187 Battersea Bridge Road, London SW11 3AS, UK
www.stpaulspublishing.com

Copyright © ST PAULS UK, 2010

ISBN 978-0-85439-792-1

A catalogue record is available for this book from the British Library.

Set by TuKan DTP, Stubbington, Fareham, UK
Printed through s|s|media, Wallington, Surrey

ST PAULS is an activity of the priests and brothers of the Society of St Paul who proclaim the Gospel through the media of social communication.

INTRODUCTION

I was born in London in 1801 and had a very happy childhood. After studying at Oxford, I became the Vicar of St Mary's and was later ordained a priest in the Catholic Church.

The Pope asked me to start an Oratory in England, which I did, in Birmingham. I spent many happy years helping people to know and love God.

When I was made a Cardinal, I chose as my motto *"Heart speaks to heart"*. As you read the story of my life in this book, I hope my heart will speak to your heart so that you too can know and love God.

My name is John Henry Newman. Today I live in the bright, shining light of Heaven, but once I lived in the world: like you.

I was born in London in 1801 and I remember when I was young, seeing everyone's windows lit up with candles after Nelson's victory at the Battle of Trafalgar. Those little lights shone in the darkness of my bedroom, and in my life God wanted me to shine with the light of truth and love.

As a boy I loved the good things God had given me: I played the violin, rode horses, rowed boats and at school edited a newspaper called 'The Spy'. I had a happy family life. I was the oldest child and had two brothers and three sisters.

When I was fifteen my father lost all his money; it wasn't his fault but we felt ashamed and had to move house. I wondered if God really cared for me, but then He touched my heart. I knew that He was calling me to follow Him alone for my whole life. God made me for a special purpose and only that mattered.

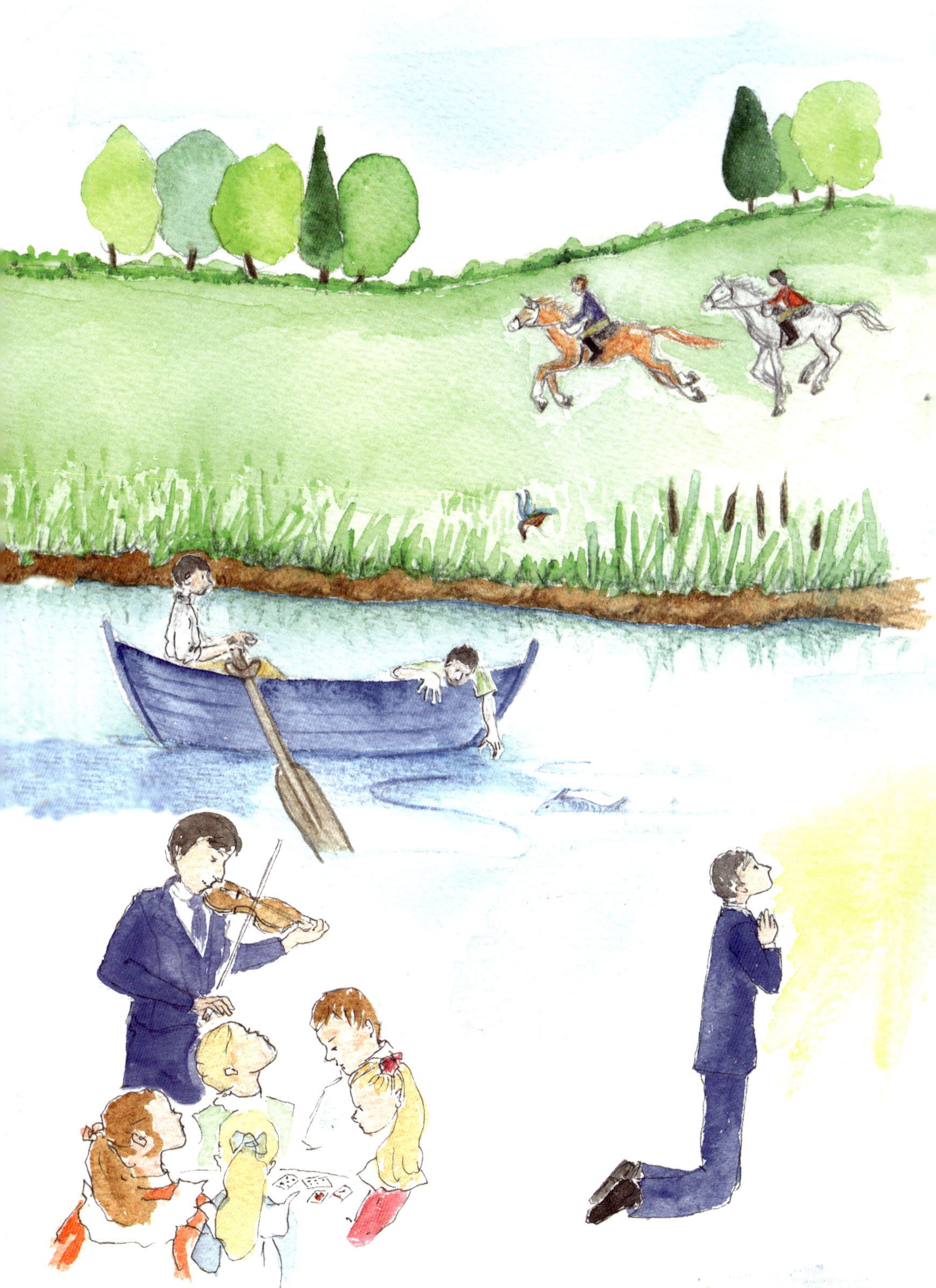

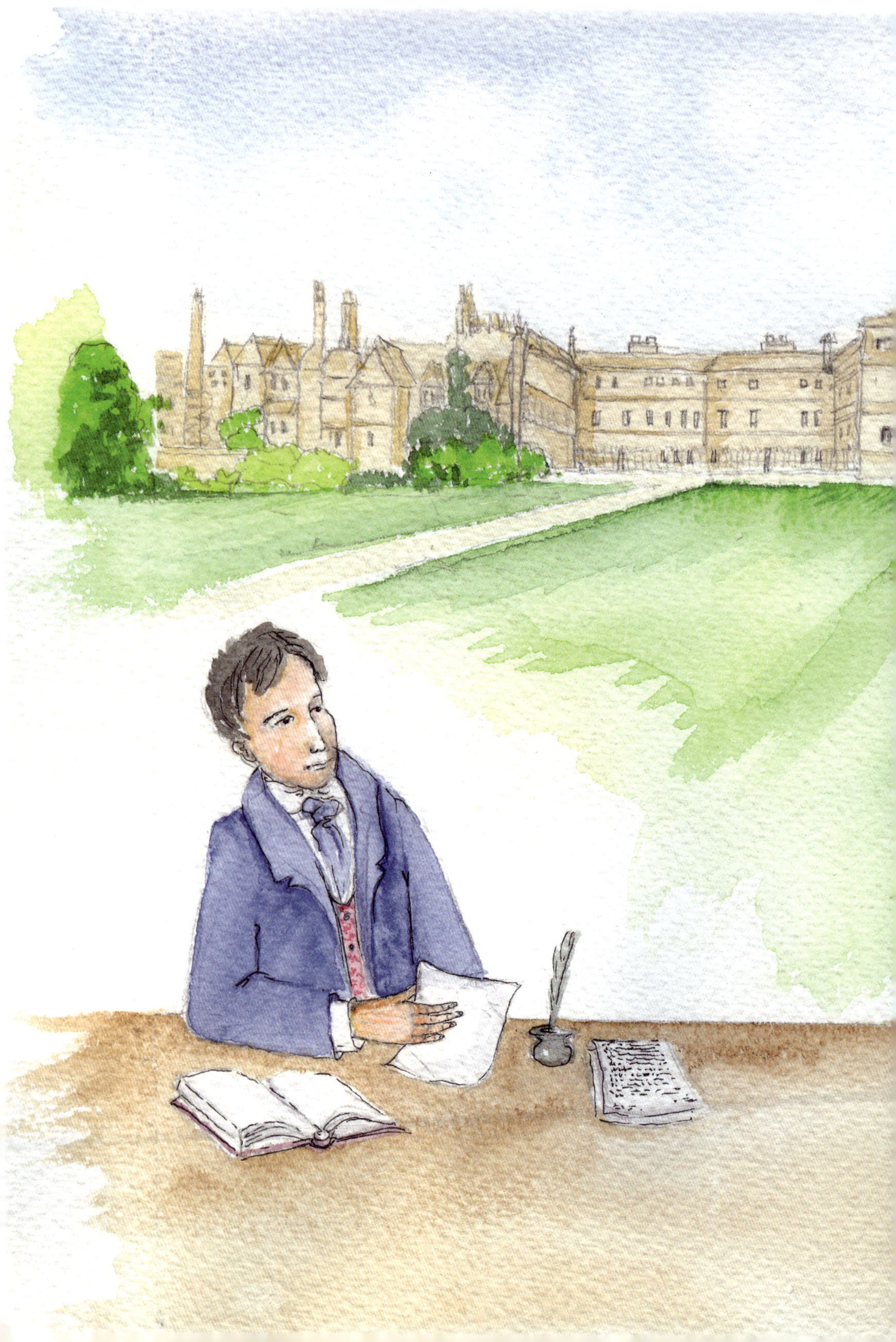

Aged sixteen, I went to Trinity College, Oxford. Oxford was so beautiful and was a whole new world to me.

I wrote to my father about the food, "Tell Mama there are gooseberry, raspberry and apricot pies!" I made very close friends at Oxford, but other people used to tease and make fun of me. I worked so hard that I fell ill and did badly in my exams. It still seemed hard to know what was God's plan for me.

I had to take an exam to become a Fellow, a teacher, at Oriel College in Oxford. This time I did so well that the Fellows of Oriel invited me to join their college. Bells rang out from three towers on that happy day. I felt very young and shy among all the clever men at Oriel but they were kind and welcomed me.

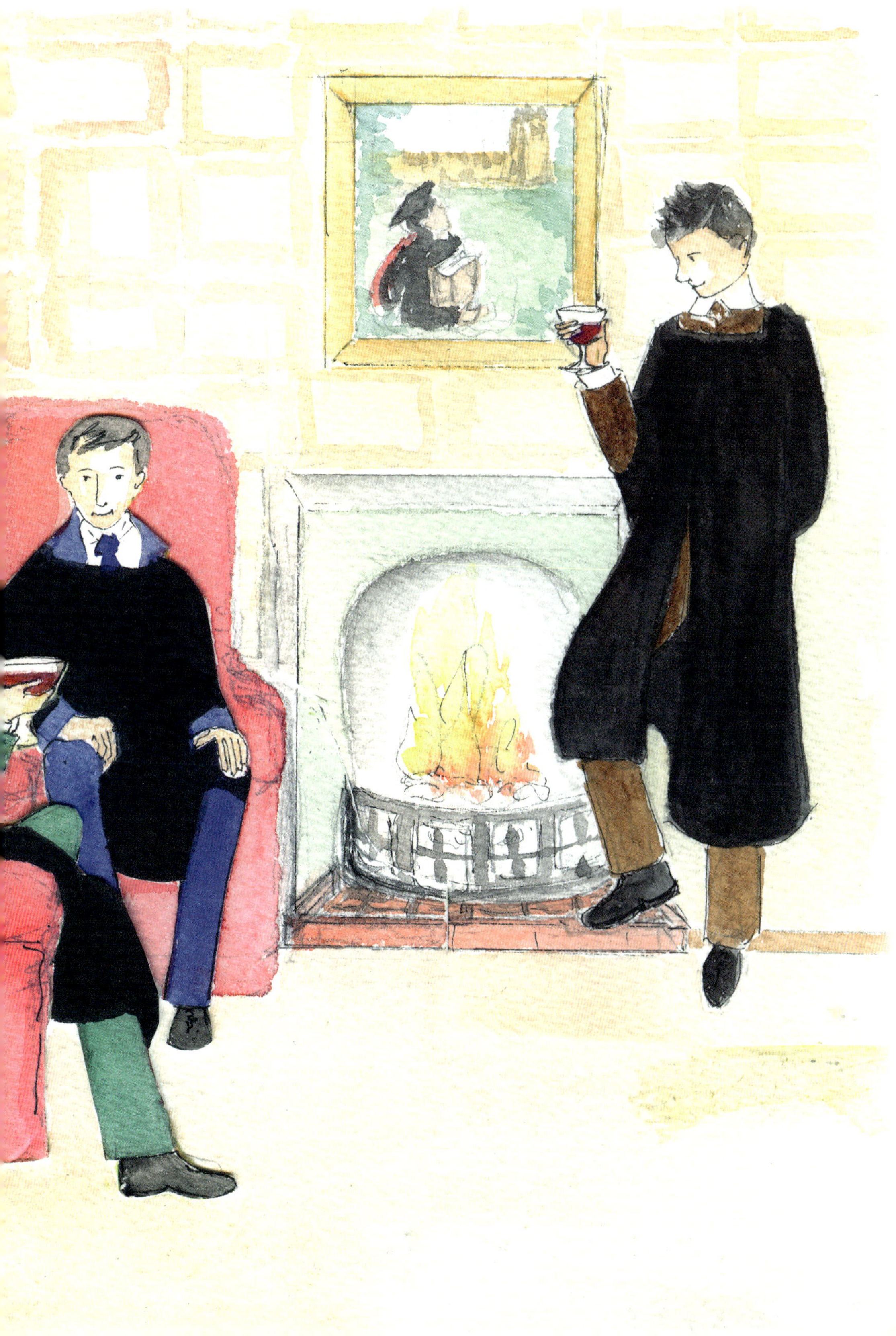

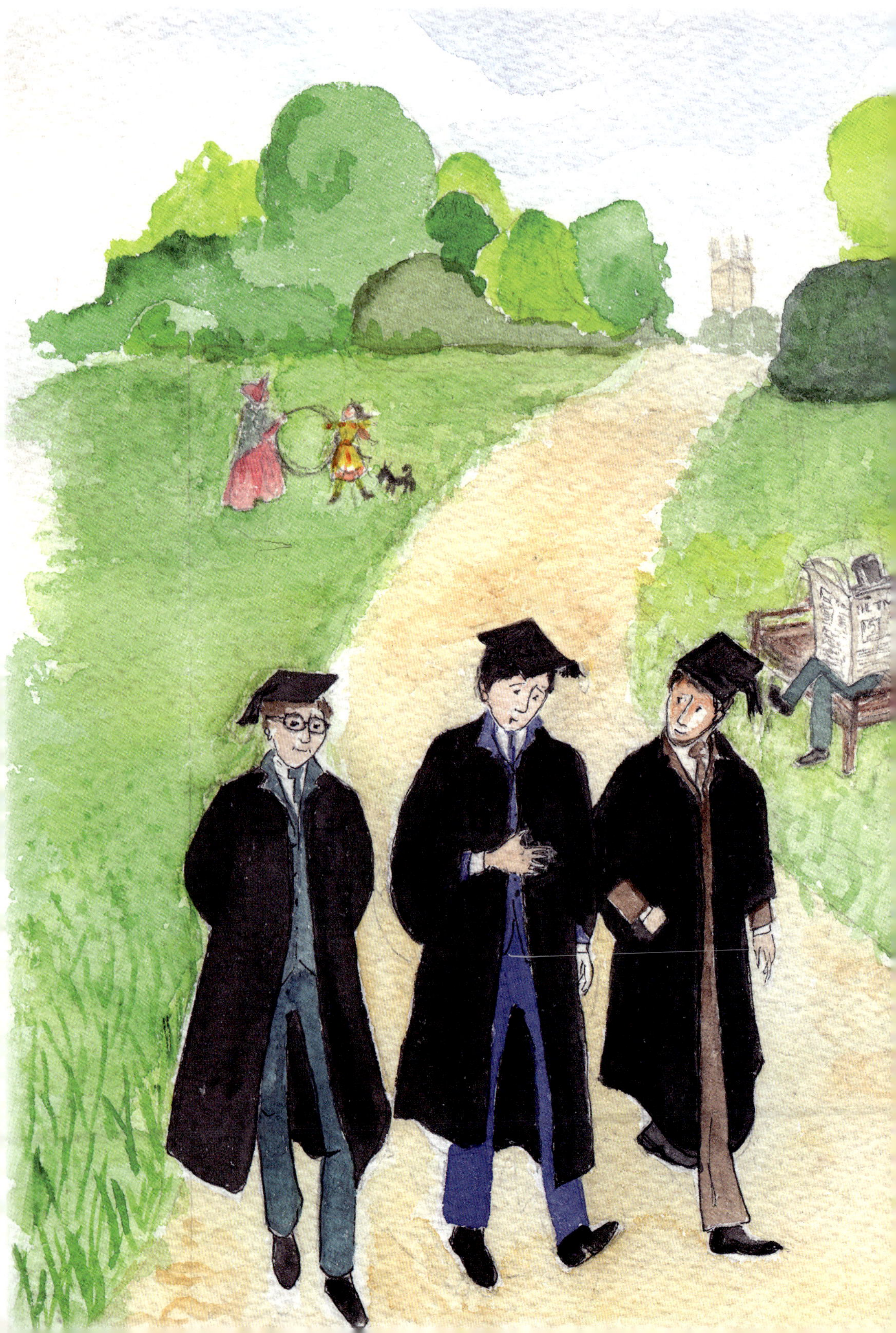

At Oxford I had the task of teaching others. I made sure that I didn't only help them to pass exams but also to love God. I discovered that the best way to do this was to be a friend to my pupils. You can learn things from books, but you learn even more when one heart speaks to another heart.

One summer I went on a long journey to Italy. It was so beautiful that I wrote to my sister Harriet that even the frogs were musical! But I fell very ill with fever. In the heat, with the fleas biting me and my whole body in pain, I thought I would die, but I knew that I had work to do in England. God would bring me back home. I wrote a poem, asking Him to keep me in His care one step at a time:

> "Lead, kindly Light...
> The night is dark and
>   I am far from home...
> One step enough for me."

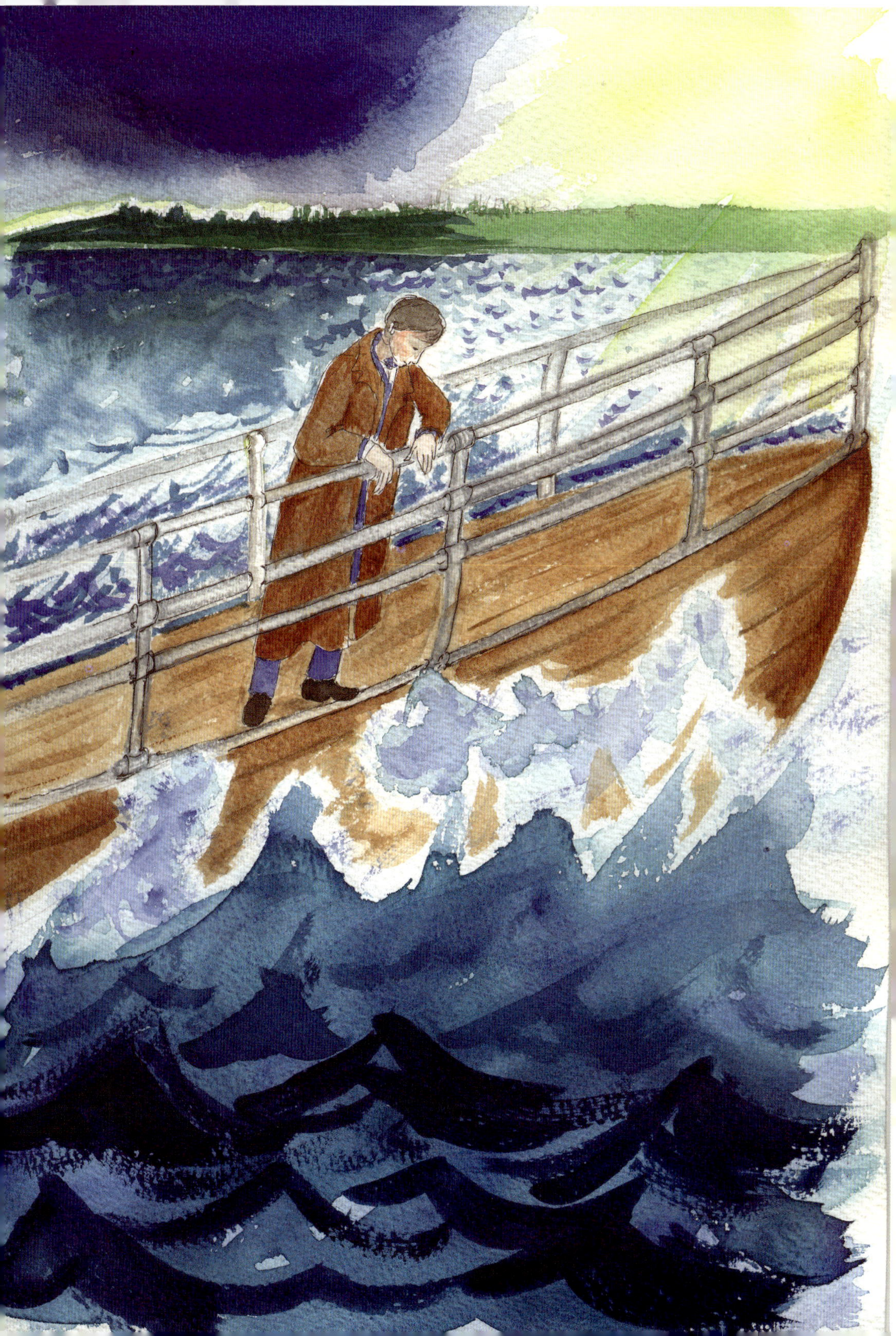

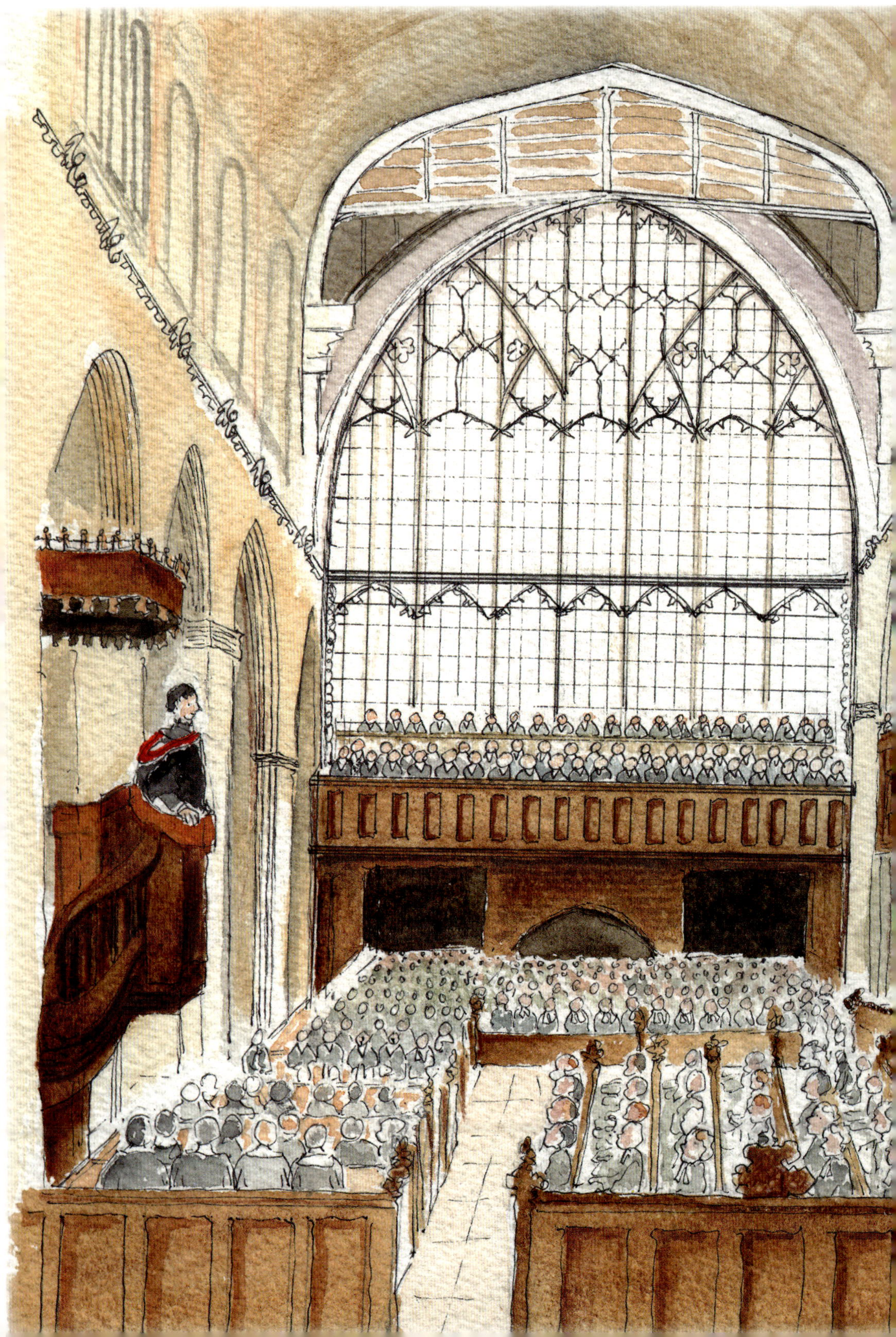

I was ordained in the Church of England and appointed Vicar of St Mary's, the University Church in Oxford.

My sermons were so popular that students had to sit on the window-sills of this big church to fit in. However, not everyone was pleased; some of the colleges moved the time of dinner to stop people from listening to me at St Mary's. The Head of my own college stopped sending me pupils to teach.

I moved to Littlemore, a small village three miles from Oxford. There I built a church and a school for the poor people. I even made sure that the girls in the school had clean, new dresses.

I lived in some old stables with some of my friends. We lived quietly, praying and reading. When I began to read books by the saints of long ago, I wondered if the kindly light of truth was leading me to the Catholic Church.

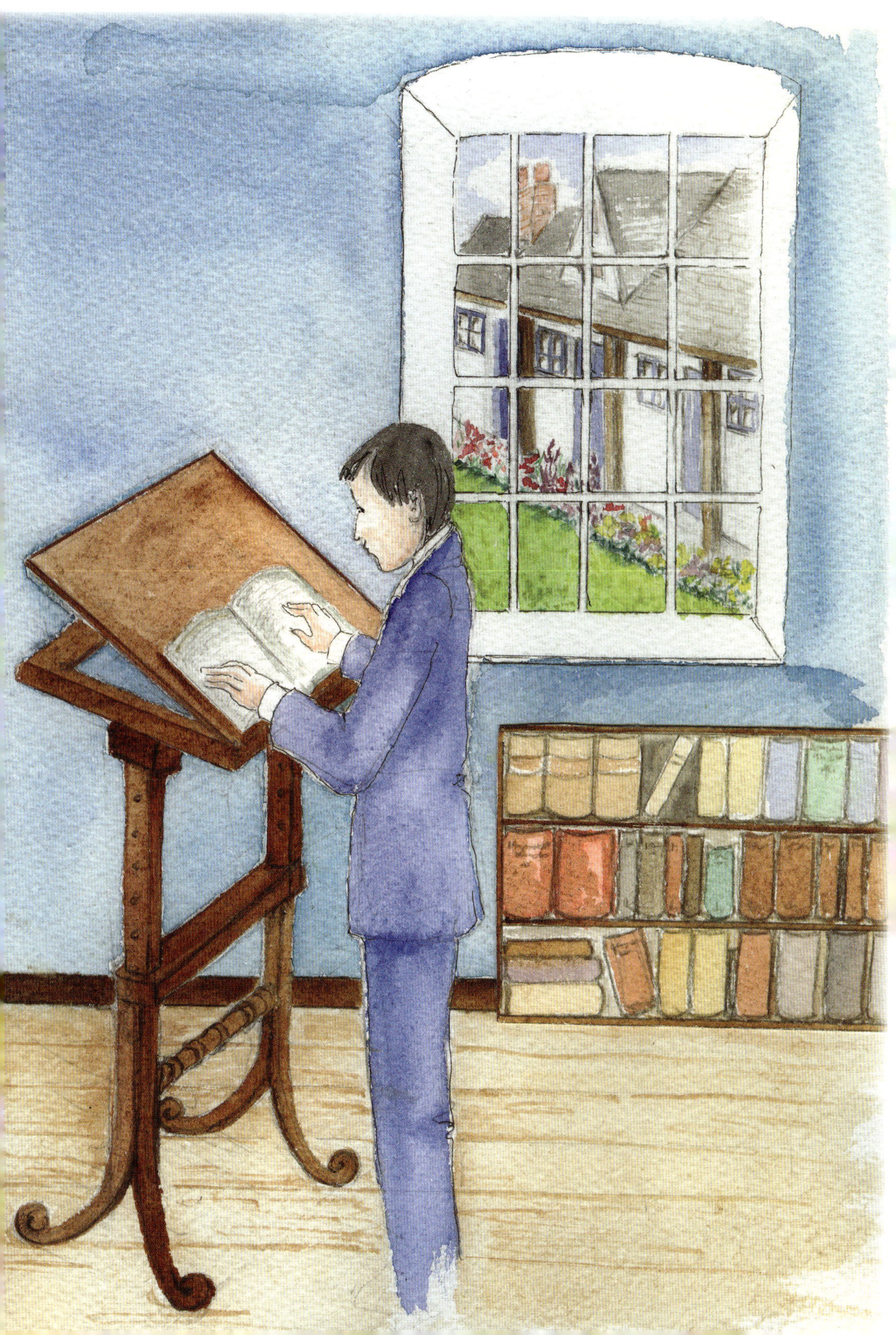

I knew that if I became a Catholic I would have to leave beautiful Oxford far behind and that many friends would never speak to me again, but a voice inside me told me this is what God wanted. I had to obey this voice.

I asked a holy priest from Italy called Father Dominic Barberi to come to Littlemore. Father Dominic arrived in the pouring rain one night in October. As he dried out by the fire I fell to my knees and asked him to make me a Catholic. The light had led me home.

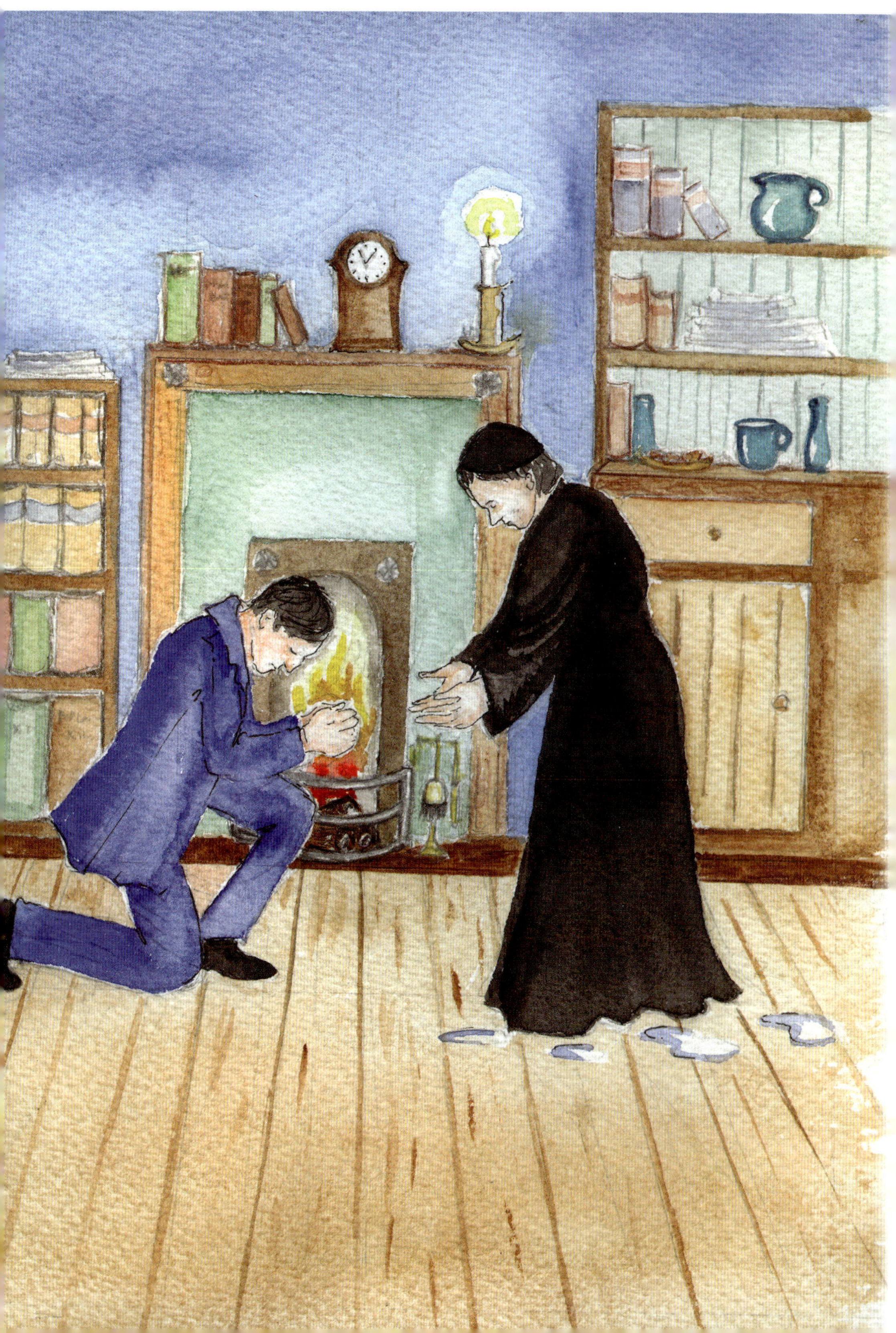

Many people were very angry that I had become a Catholic. One of my sisters ignored me for the rest of her life but I felt as though I had come into port after a rough sea voyage. I could receive Jesus in Holy Communion, and that made up for everything.

At the age of 44 I went to Rome and became a student again so that I could be a priest. I learnt about a Roman saint called Philip Neri, who was full of joy. Philip had formed a group of priests called the Oratory. After I was ordained, the Pope asked me to start an Oratory of Saint Philip in England.

I arrived back in England as a priest and went to Maryvale, near Birmingham. Together with other friends we started the English Oratory and asked Mary to be our mother and helper. People in England weren't used to seeing priests in the street or hearing them called, "Father". Sometimes they shouted at us, or said that we kept prisoners in our cellars! But we went to care for the poor people of Birmingham.

There was a sickness called the plague at Bilston and two of us from the Oratory went to help. Happily, the sickness ended before we arrived.

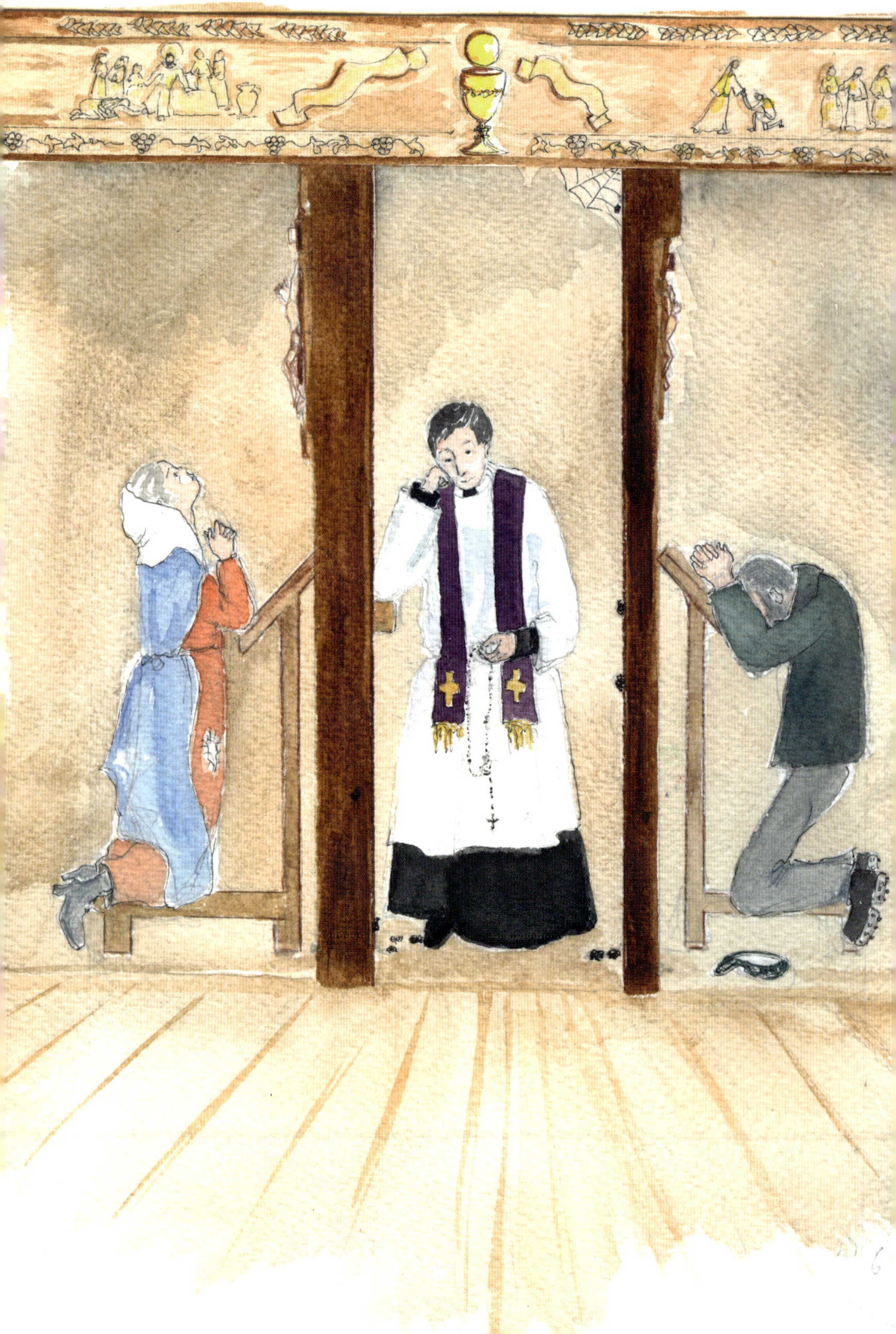

An Oratory is a place of prayer, where the priests of the Oratory stay in one place for their whole life. They say Mass, hear confessions and teach people to pray. They make friends with people to help them to love God.

Our first church was an old gin shop and, when I heard confessions, I was half-eaten by bugs!

I also wrote hymns and played music to lead people to Jesus.

This is a verse from my famous hymn:

> "Praise to the Holiest in the height
> And in the depth be praise;
> In all His words most wonderful
> Most sure in all His ways!"

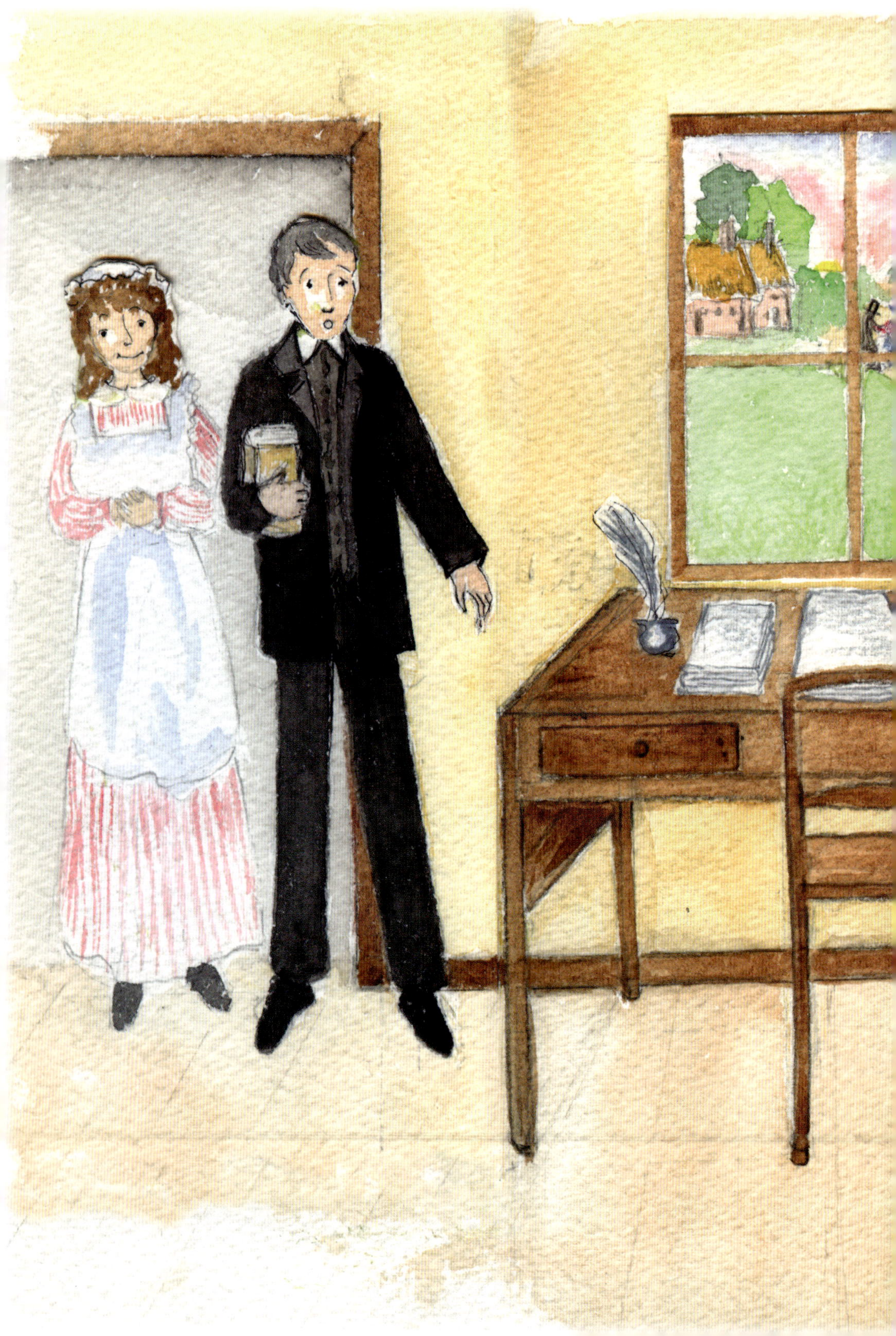

The bishops in Ireland asked me to start a University in Dublin. This meant that I went back and forth across the sea to Ireland so many times.

During this time I kept on writing books and letters all day at my writing desk. One day I came back to my room in Dublin and the maid had tidied all my papers...into size order!

I started a school for boys at the Birmingham Oratory. I still played my violin and helped the boys to act in plays. I had to write reports to their parents who were sometimes worried that their sons ate too much cake!

The boys at the Oratory School called me "Old Jack" and I made sure that the school made them ready to do well in this world, but more importantly to look towards heaven. Through friendship and kindness I taught my pupils how to be good Christians.

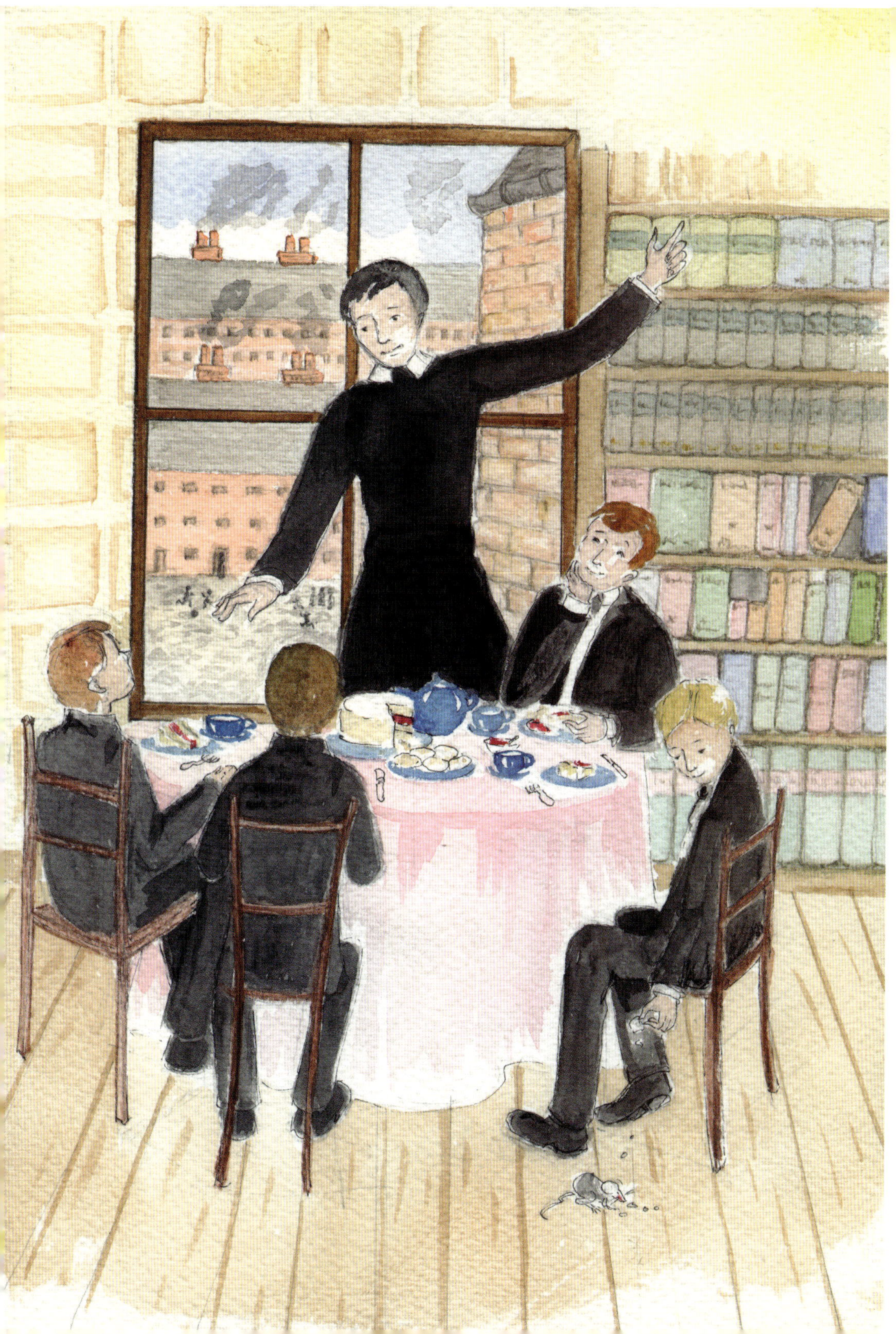

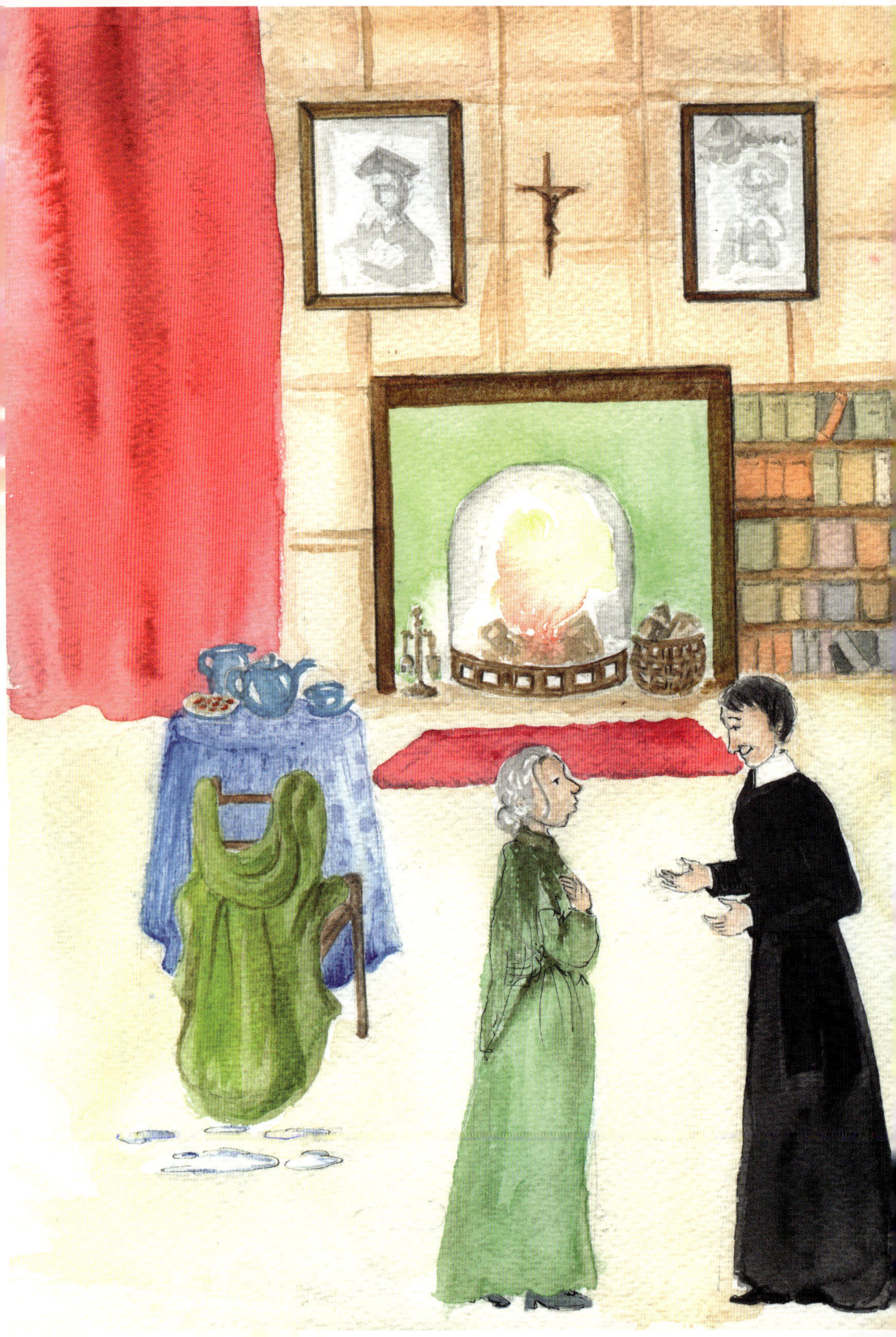

To show people that I meant to follow Jesus, I wrote down the story of my life, in fact I was always writing. People from all over the world would write to me asking for my advice and I wrote back to help them.

One woman came to the Oratory and wasn't sure whether she should become a Catholic. When I helped her dry out by the fire and spoke to her kindly, she knew that God wanted her to join the Church.

In my old age I became very popular. The Pope asked me to become a Cardinal. I was worried I would have to leave my friends (the other Fathers of the Oratory) but the Pope gave me special permission to stay in Birmingham.

I had to choose a Cardinal's motto in Latin: *"Cor ad Cor Loquitur"*, which means, "Heart speaks to heart". When people read my books, my heart speaks to their heart.

❦ lived on until I was ninety. The last time I ever went out was in the snow to speak to the Catholic workers at Cadbury's, the chocolate factory. At my funeral, in 1890, thousands of people came to say goodbye. God's kindly light had led me home to heaven.

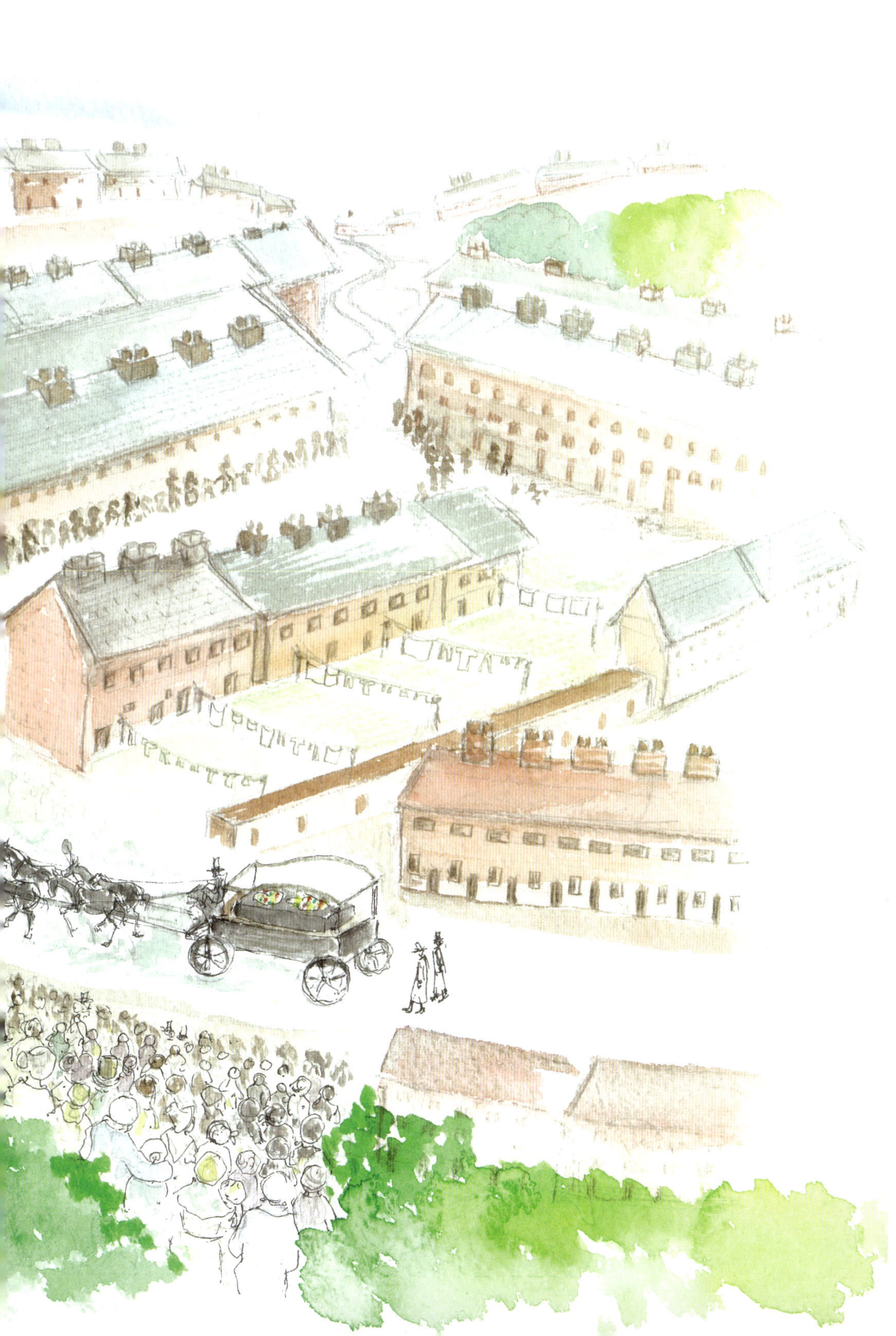

My books and letters still help people to love God today.

A man in America called Jack Sullivan prayed to me when he was in hospital and he got better. God had worked a miracle!

So Pope Benedict decided that I could be called Blessed John Henry Newman. So *you* can ask for my help too. Together we can follow the light of Jesus wherever it leads.

I told people that God wants us all to be saints.

You might think that saints are all people from long ago in story books.

But the only way to become a saint is to do the duties of each day perfectly. When someone does that, they shine with the light of Jesus. You can do that too!

What was the name of the ship Nelson captained at the Battle of Trafalgar?

_____

_____

_____

At which college in Oxford was Newman a teacher?

_____

_____

_____

What are the first words of the poem Newman wrote in Italy?

_____

_____

_____

What is the name of the saint who started the Oratory?

_____

_____

_____

What was the name of the Pope who made Newman a Cardinal?

_____

_____

In which three English cities can you find an Oratory?

_____

_____

_____

Praise to the Holiest in the height,
and in the depth be praise;
in all his words most wonderful,
most sure in all his ways!

O loving wisdom of our God!
When all was sin and shame,
a second Adam to the fight
and to the rescue came.

O wisest love! that flesh and blood,
which did in Adam fail,
should strive afresh against the foe,
should strive, and should prevail.

And that a higher gift of grace
should flesh and blood refine:
God's presence and his very self,
and essence all-divine.

O generous love! that he who smote
in Man for man the foe,
the double agony in Man
for man should undergo.

And in the garden secretly,
and on the cross on high,
should teach his brethren, and inspire
to suffer and to die.

Praise to the Holiest in the height,
and in the depth be praise;
in all his words most wonderful,
most sure in all his ways!

~~~

O God, who bestowed on the Priest
Blessed John Henry Newman
the grace to follow your kindly light and find
peace in your Church;
graciously grant that, through his intercession
and example, we may be led out of shadows
and images, into the fullness of your truth.
Through our Lord Jesus Christ, your Son,
who lives and reigns with you in the unity of
the Holy Spirit, one God, for ever and ever.
Amen.

May He support us all the day long,
till the shades lengthen and the evening comes,
and the busy world is hushed,
and the fever of life is over,
and our work is done.
Then in His mercy may He give us a safe lodging,
and a holy rest.
Amen.

~~~